Living With
The
Unexpected

Living With The Unexpected

Barry Bailey

Abingdon Press • Nashville

Living with the Unexpected

Copyright © 1984 by Abingdon Press

Library of Congress Cataloging in Publication Data

BAILEY, BARRY, 1926–
   Living with the unexpected.
   1. Methodist Church--Sermons. 2. Sermons, American.
I. Title.
BX8333.B24L57 1984   252'.076   83-15692

ISBN 0-687-22366-0

MANUFACTURED BY THE PARTHENON PRESS AT
NASHVILLE, TENNESSEE, UNITED STATES OF AMERICA

*This book is dedicated, with deep appreciation,
to our television audience.*

Contents

Preface

What I have tried to do in this book is to invite you to join me in looking at some ideas that may be beneficial to us in everyday life. We are all so very much alike, and we need about all the help we can get.

Many of us want security without monotony and change without shock, and all along the way we know what it is to experience the unexpected.

I want to express my deep appreciation to Eugenia Hinds, my secretary; to Gloria Degani, who assists in editing my sermons; and to Gail Cooke, who has worked with me again on this book, the fourth that I have done for Abingdon.

Also, I am deeply appreciative of my wife, Joan, and our children, Barry K. and Janice, the congregation of First United Methodist Church of Fort Worth, and the audience that worships with us by way of television.

What About Faith?

Isn't it interesting that so often fear is associated with everyday life, while faith is thought of in terms of a religious experience. Actually, we have faith daily, but we tend to correlate it with a church or with God. As a matter of fact, we cannot live without faith in something. The idea of faith per se may not excite us, but we are definitely interested in the results we think faith can produce. Whether it pertains to religion or not, all of us have faith and frequently we try to prove our faith.

Simon Peter made his living as a fisherman. One day, when Jesus was quite popular, throngs of people surrounded him. So he went aboard Simon Peter's boat and continued to speak to the people from the boat. Then he turned to Simon Peter and said, "Launch out into deep water." Maybe he did that simply because he wanted the fishermen to go out where the fish were, or perhaps he had been with people for so long that he needed a respite from the crowds. We can understand that. You cannot continue to give yourself unless you receive. For whatever reason, Jesus said, "Launch out into the deep, and let down your nets." Simon Peter replied, "We have toiled all night and we have not caught anything; but nevertheless, if you say so we will do this." They went out into deeper water, put down their nets, and caught so many fish that the nets began to break. They gathered the fish into the boat, and the boat began to sink.

We can look at this story and think, "That's marvelous; Simon Peter listened to Jesus, and look at how many fish they caught!" I think those fishermen went a little too far—why break their nets? Solving one problem created another; their boat began to sink. They did not use very good judgment, did they? Perhaps they were carried away by greed. For years I have felt that if you cannot improve on a story, why tell it? I am not saying that this story was tampered with, but somewhere along the line it seems to have been a little overdone. First, the fishermen were not catching any fish, then they had so many fish that their boat began to sink. The central idea of the story is obvious: "Believe in Jesus and you will catch fish." That is basically how the churches saw it. But from that perspective you are bragging about fish, not faith.

What was Jesus trying to tell these disciples? Let me suggest one possibility. He was going to go for broke one day, and it seems to me that he was warning Simon Peter: "The time is going to come when I will ask you to move out into the deep and you will, but you will not catch anything. I am going to ask you to risk your life in faith on some things that may never happen, but they are vital." His words could have several implications perhaps, but one thing I believe he is saying is, "Your faith must go beyond your proof."

Yet you and I want a faith that works, that proves itself. Why else, we think, would we have faith? "Believe in God and make things happen the way we want them to happen" is the way we often look at faith. If that is not true, we ask, why should we believe in God, and of what benefit is faith to us anyway?

Sometime ago I was preaching in Oklahoma and had an enjoyable visit with a lady who had come to the service with several other members of her church. They watch our television services regularly, so she feels like a member of our congregation, as well as her own. Toward the end of our conversation, she said, "Barry, I would like you to come out and look at my car." So I did. She told me that she had been alone in that car, not long before, when it was thrown around in a terrible storm—strong winds, high water, and hail—that battered and dented the car. She had been afraid she would be killed, but she said that she began to think about some of the things I had preached, and she said, "I do agree with your theology, but at that terrifying moment I thought, 'Oh, I hope Barry Bailey is wrong and God intervenes now and gets me out of this!'" I would agree with her.

She survived that experience and she is safe. She should thank God. But, you see, if we expect God to rescue us on demand, the time will come when we need to be rescued and it will not happen.

If we go far enough in life, we will pray for something we want desperately, having faith in God that we will receive it. If that is our reasoning, think how we can behave toward others. We may mean well, but, with that mind frame, we can go to someone who is ill and say, "If you had more faith, you would be be well. If you had more faith, you never would have been sick in the first place. God is trying to tell you something. I don't know what it is, but examine your life, clean it up; something is wrong." If someone said that to us, we could always find something wrong, something we thought we needed to rectify, could we not? If you have a problem—an illness, difficulties with your work, or whatever else—God is not trying to tell you something through a disaster. God is not that kind of God. Nevertheless, we want a faith that will get God on our side. We want a God who can act, a God who can do something, a God who can prove himself.

Recently, I read a very interesting biography which dealt with a family. In one short passage the author talked about himself and revealed something of his own life. He mentioned that he never really had a family, never saw his father, that he could remember. He saw his mother only a few times. He grew up in a foster home, but he never felt a part of that group. The people in that home had very little to give him materially. They tried to give him love, but they did not know how. That was his family until he was seventeen years old. He said that in the back of his mind he always had a feeling that he was there only because they were paid to care for him. He could have imagined that; perhaps they did much better than he could comprehend, but that was his understanding of the experience.

During World War II, when he was seventeen, he enlisted in the Navy. On the day that he was to leave, he went to the bus station alone, not expecting anyone to see him off, but the woman who had been his seventh-grade teacher knew he was leaving that day, and she came to hug him and say goodbye. He said that for the first time in his life he felt what it was to have someone love him.

There must have been many times when he was a small boy that he prayed, "O God, help me; I want a family like others have." I imagine that on occasion he felt guilty and thought, "If I had more faith my life would be different. I am being punished." Isn't that what the church says in a conventional sense? "If you have enough faith in God, He will do everything you want; you can even move mountains with such a faith." We know that is not so, for one reason because it didn't work for Jesus. Who could have had more faith than he did? Yet he said from the cross, "My God, why have you forsaken me?" We can build our lives, believing that if we have enough faith in God, we can persuade him to come and do what we want him to do. However, just when we have our lives ironed out like that, and everything nailed down in its proper place, we are surprised; shocked; the unexpected takes place.

Think of Simon Peter again. He had fished all night and had not caught a thing, but Jesus went aboard his boat, and look what happened. Jesus said, "Go out into the deep; put down your nets and fish again." And Simon Peter replied, "We have tried all night long." In a way he was saying, "This is foolish, but because you have asked me to do it, I will." So they put out their nets and they caught a lot of fish. Do you think that God put the fish there and told Jesus where to have them fish in order to impress the fishermen? Did God say, "We are going to show Simon Peter how smart we are, Jesus; we are going to show him that if he has faith in you he will come out ahead"? I do not know what actually happened, but I would imagine that Jesus had a good eye and knew there were fish farther out. He knew they traveled in schools. I am not implying that he was a better fisherman than Simon Peter; but often when we know something well our very knowledge and awareness may blind us to a possibility. Someone else may readily see what we have overlooked. I would imagine Jesus knew there were fish out there. "Go on out and try again," he said. And the men caught a lot of fish.

They rejoiced because of their catch, but the day will come when they can hear Jesus say very clearly, "I want you to rejoice because you have faith, faith in things that go beyond any kind of proof." Look at the problems in the world. Many are insoluble. And, more personally, there comes a time when we are faced with a dilemma, we are hurt, and we pray, "O God, help me; I must make it through today, through this week; what shall I do?" Then, perhaps our problem is solved. We may say, "O God, I have faith and my worry is over, and I am content."

I hope we don't stop there; that is like being elated over a large catch of fish. Is that as far as we are going to grow? There are problems in our neighborhoods. What about our cities? What about the problems in our state, our nation, our world? Hopefully we love America, but I hope our love is broad enough to include the whole human race. Are we so naïve that we assume America can be strong and, if necessary, bomb other people to bits and then thank God for it?

We have been called Christians. We are observing one of the most creative minds there ever was, and the person who took many risks. And I think Jesus taught, "Now, Simon Peter, launch out into the deep and put out your nets and you will catch some fish. I know you will rejoice because you have a good catch, but I am talking about faith. There will be a time when I will push you as far as you can go; push you to gamble for things the world cannot even see, but that the world so desperately needs."

Jesus had an eye; he knew that perhaps there were fish in deeper water. Oh, but he has an eye that sees farther than that, much farther—he can see things we have never experienced, but that we say we want. What do you think keeps us from getting them? Why is life not better? Do you think God is holding these things back? Of course not! We know better than we are willing to live; we know more than we are willing to practice. We rationalize and justify our smallness time and time again. We will continue to do that, then someday we will die and be gone and others will take our place. But if we do not leave them some improved

21

ideas, and if they fail to take more risks, what will happen to the human race, ultimately? Go out into the deep.

It is of the utmost importance that we understand that faith does not necessarily bring us what we want. Faith in God is not an assurance that we will always receive what we desire. We should know that from our own experience. As a matter of fact, the more faith we have in God, the more we may be disappointed. But continue to have faith. The danger in having faith and receiving solutions to inconsequential difficulties is that we may never move beyond that. We may say, "God, thank you for solving my problems." Then we may become selfish and think, "God, I wanted a better job and now I have it, and I don't owe anything to anyone else." What about our responsibility to life and society, to our community?

Television commercials, to me, are enjoyable at times. One favorite of mine advertises a camera. In the commercial, a couple is looking at a picture they have taken, and the woman says to the man, "There he is in his cowboy outfit." Another woman looks at the picture and says, "Yes, and the horses just hate it." Next we see two older women, sitting looking at their photos, and one of them inspects a picture of the other woman and comments, "It's a great picture; it makes you look twenty years younger." The other woman surveys herself, and says, "Twenty won't do it!" There are times when we feel, "I need more help than that." There is no way we can have faith enough in God to assure us that we will always get what we want.

Perhaps that is as it should be, because the truth is that faith is more important than the accomplishment. Catching those fish—what did that mean? It meant that Simon Peter and the others caught some fish and that's about all it signified. Undoubtedly, they caught fish in days to come without a word from Jesus. Their catch meant that they were good fishermen. Faith is important, regardless of what is accomplished. Suppose I am sick and I have faith in God; I want to recover and I do get well. That is fine. But some day I will become ill and I will not recover. What is important—the faith or the recovery? Both, perhaps, but in the final analysis it is the faith. Have faith in what ought to be, whether it happens or not.

I have special admiration for teachers, and there is no group of teachers I admire more than those who work with exceptional children, children with noticeable handicaps. What reward is there for a teacher working with a child who is severely handicapped? The child may never learn to read well, may never be well coordinated, may never be able to walk very well. Where is the joy? What is the return for the teacher? Does she do it for some obvious estimable goal? At times, can she see that she has made great progress—is that why she does it? If so, she may as well stop. Why does she do it? She does it because it is right, because a human soul is involved, because of some intangibles that cannot be measured. And always, I think, the faith is more important than the accomplishment.

Sometime ago a singer of international renown came to our area to perform. A cook in the hotel where the singer stayed had admired the singer all of her life, but the cook had never met the singer or heard her perform in person. Some of the hotel employees decided to do something nice for the singer—surprise her one morning with a special breakfast. When they knocked on her door with the breakfast, the singer was indignant that anyone would disturb her that early in the morning, and it was not all that early. She angrily called the hotel manager, threatening to leave.

Of course, she had every right to sleep as late as she wished, and she was under no obligation to accept the breakfast if she did not want it. Her contract contained no stipulations about breakfast in a certain city. She was completely within her rights in responding as she did. Yet, how do we react to this story? When that singer walks on stage, we can enjoy her performance. She is not required to be polite to people. We would rather hear her sing, although she may not be cordial, than listen to someone who is gracious but cannot sing.

What of the cook in the hotel kitchen? Perhaps since childhood she had thought, "I'd like to do something significant with my life," and maybe gradually, due to this desire, she began to live vicariously through the lives of others. Then the day came when she had an opportunity to do something nice for an important star whom she admired. It seemed like a good idea—thoughtful, a friendly gesture—to prepare a special breakfast and surprise the singer with it, but the cook was rejected. And, what do you think was the result? She might have thought, "I will not reach out any more. When you are nice to people they just slap you down." We can make the same decision because all of us have had similar experiences. Haven't you loved and been rejected? Haven't you cared for someone who hurt you? Haven't you tried to work toward some goal and wound up looking like a fool, appearing altruistic, almost to the point of naïveté?

In this incident, whether the singer accepted the breakfast or rejected it is not important. What is significant is that one person cared enough about another to express that care by preparing a special breakfast for her. The attitude of caring is what matters. Do not let the world beat you down. It tried that with Jesus. If Jesus had had faith only in proportion to his accomplishments, he would have had no more faith than we have. But his faith was not like that. "Are you going to leave me, too?" he asked his disciples. He had faith in God and he was nailed to a cross. He loved people and they walked away. We have faith in substantive things—friendship, love, world peace, harmony, forgiveness. Whether any of them are ever translated into reality is not the issue.

Jesus, I believe, literally calls us to take risks for the most impossible things in the world. As Christians we are supposed to live for some things that the world has only experienced in a limited way. We are supposed to go out into the deep—I mean this. Who do you expect to change the concept of the world? Who are you going to leave it up to? We are neither more intelligent than nor superior to other people, but we are following a leader who asks us to risk for seeming impossibilities. If we are only kind to those who are kind to us, what difference does that make? Jesus told us that quite clearly. We love America, but someone needs to love the whole world. We love our race, but someone needs to care for all of humanity.

It is my belief that Jesus calls us to have faith in some things that we may never find—world peace, a solution to world hunger. Surely, in a local church situation, when food is given to needy families, we realize that we are not making much of a dent in world hunger. But the alternative would be to become so practical that we stop helping anyone. When we are of help to one person, do we expect to change anything worldwide? Not really. But we should never minimize our act of kindness, no matter how small its impact may seem.

Jesus knew what he was talking about; he was not teaching Simon Peter how to fish. That is not faith, but that is what we want to boast about. "Believe in Jesus and you get fish." Jesus was teaching Simon Peter how to live. "Simon Peter, you may think you are in deep water now, but I am going to take you into some really deep water, and it will cost you everything you have. I am going to ask you to go as far as you can, and farther, and to live for some things that matter. Would you prefer to be applauded by a crowd that praises you when you are wrong, or would you rather risk, in faith? Someone has to take a risk and move out into the deep."

My suggestion is not that we become converted and come to Jesus. No doubt we have done that, maybe several times. I am going much farther than that. In your minds, think some bigger thoughts; you know what they are. Let us not brag about faith when we are really talking about fishing. Instead, let us risk our lives for God through Christ by caring for his world and its people.

Ways of Pleasing God

All of us are born with one innate fear, and that is the fear of being dropped. We enter this life apprehensively, with the inherent emotional capacity to be afraid of being dropped. On the other hand, a desire to be held is not born in us; we come into this world with a negative consciousness. Neither society nor our parents make a knowing effort to teach us this negative concept; it comes from the whole matrix of life. That may or may not explain why so much of our religion stems from a less than positive idea.

This negative approach is evidenced by many of us when somewhere in the process of our growth we begin to think God is standing against us. Better mend our ways, we think, or he will get us and we will go to hell. We are not sure what will keep us from hell, but we want to avoid it, whatever it takes. We think we'd better be "good" enough, but we can't; we think we should have the right faith, but we don't know how. We are afraid. We join what we hope is the right church, associating with people we think may have found an answer, and then we evoke that idea in ourselves. We are found; we are saved. We know we have found what has been eluding us. The truth is that we had what we were seeking all along, not because of who we are or what we do, but because of what God is.

God is love always. But the world really has not known that. I don't know it either. I preach it and I write it, but I don't know it. How long must we hear something before we understand it, or be exposed to it before we see it? How often must we repeat it before we consciously absorb it?

Some eight hundred years before the birth of Jesus, a prophet appeared on the scene. Perhaps he was self-appointed; there is nothing wrong with that. When a job needs to be done, why does someone decide that he is the one to do it? Because it needs to be done. Is it necessary to have irrefutable proof that someone is called from "out there" to do what is "in here"? Elijah stood before King Ahab and said, "Since you are making sacrifices to Baal and not worshipping as you should, there will not be rain in this land until I say so." He was assuming a great deal of authority. It is one thing to become a prophet, it is something else to speak for God, and it is yet another thing to think you are God. Elijah began at the top by declaring, "It is not going to rain until I let it rain." To make matters even more impressive, it did not rain for about three years. The drought made Ahab angry; I don't blame him. It was dry for such a long time, so he began to search for the prophet Elijah. He wanted to discuss the situation with him because he thought he was being cursed by God.

We are like Ahab. Regardless of how perceptive or intelligent we are, there are times some questions haunt us: "What have I done to cause this? What is God trying to tell me? Look at the sequence of events in my life. Have they occurred because I have sinned or made mistakes, or is God just against me?" When something good happens to us we attribute it to God. Certainly we should be thankful when something good happens to us, but God does not sit in heaven and decide to dispense favors, pulling strings as if we were puppets.

Elijah was speaking for God; Elijah was angry at King Ahab. He was not witnessing for God; Elijah was witnessing for himself, when he said, "I tell you, I'm going to win; my side is going to win. You are worshipping Baal." At that time the difference between Baal and Yahweh was almost microscopic; both were considered war gods. The followers of Baal evidenced their devotion by killing people; Yahweh's adherents showed their faithfulness by killing people. Here the difference between the two sets of followers was found only in semantics, expressions.

Historically, we find people trying to please God. How do we think we can please God? One of the first things we notice when we read the story of Elijah is the fact that he thought he could please God by eliminating bad people. Aren't we like that? And who are the bad people? It is easy to identify them—they are the ones who disagree with us. Elijah was sure he was right; therefore, if he was right it must follow that anyone who disagreed with him was wrong. So he had the prophets of Baal killed—all 450 of them.

33

Before that, Elijah had met with the people and said, "You build an altar to Baal, and I also want you to build an altar to Yahweh, my God. You call for fire to come down from heaven and consume your altar and if it does, that is a sign that Baal is God. If it does not, I will call for fire to come down from heaven to consume my altar to God. If it does, then Jehovah is God." And so they built an altar to Baal and nothing happened.

And then Elijah did something that seems boorish and insensitive to me. Remember that there had been no rain for a long time; people and animals were dying. Water was precious. Yet Elijah insisted, "Get barrels of water and pour them on the altar to God. I want to show you that when God acts, he can do it with wet wood." So four barrels of water were poured on the altar, and then he told them to do it two more times. When water is plentiful, it doesn't seem wasteful to use it for whatever purpose we wish, does it? But if people and animals are dying because of lack of water, this is an unthinking, cruel thing to do. At times we can waste what is precious to someone else while at the same time giving the impression that we live religiously. Who are we fooling?

Apparently he did not consider how important water was to those people. Elijah was saying, "I want to show you how God works. God has caused this long drought because you did not worship properly. God let your babies die because you did not worship as you should. So pour water on my altar to God and I will show you the true God." They did as he said, Elijah prayed, and the altar was consumed by fire. He was so elated by his success that he had the 450 prophets of Baal killed.

Is that how we are supposed to please God, by getting rid of the bad people, those who disagree with us? We see nations view other nations in that light. How long can we continue to assume that in order for America to exist, other nations must either agree with us or be annihilated? Do you believe the world is so small that there can be room for only one idea? Is there just one economic approach? Must everyone believe in free enterprise or capitalism?

People matter; whatever can help people matters. Anything that destroys people is wrong. I say this not as an American, but as a human being. Do you think our strength lies in military might? If that were so, Rome might still exist as it did centuries ago. Strength lies in an idea. I believe communism is one of the worst menaces in the history of the world. How can we battle communism? If it could ever be done well, we might do it by combating one idea against another. I realize that we need armaments to protect ourselves, but to what extent? What do you think would really threaten communism? An idea—a philosophy— would.

In other instances, I think we attempt to please God by showing our success. When I speak of our great church, relating how much we have grown, with accompanying statistics to prove it, perhaps I am trying to impress myself, or our members, or maybe other people. But what do we really think matters? Is our success pleasing to God? If a young boy who belongs to this church is frightened and worried, do you think he cares that we have over eight thousand members or a budget of a few million dollars? Do you really think those things are of consequence to him? Of course not! I don't blame him; I'd be on his side. He is anxious and afraid, his life matters to him; he is not selfish or petty. He is like we are; he is normal. What is important to him is whatever affects his own personal life, and that is also important to God. But we are inclined to attempt to please God by showing how much success we have, flexing our muscles, and displaying our might.

Elijah went alone to the top of the hill. Ahab sent some men to look for him. Finally, fifty men reached Elijah and asked him to come down from the mountain. Displaying his might, Elijah replied, "If I am of God, let fire consume you." And, according to the story, fire destroyed them. Ahab persuaded fifty more people to approach Elijah—I don't know where he found the second fifty; I doubt they were volunteers. Nonetheless, they stood before Elijah and said, "Ahab wants to see you; come down from the mountain." And again Elijah said, "If I am of God, let fire come down and destroy you." And he wiped out those fifty also. Then fifty more men were found to go—that was really an accomplishment! But this time the leader did not ask Elijah to come down; he knelt and prayed and almost worshiped Elijah. He begged him or prayed for him to come down, and Elijah said he would.

Do you believe God burned those people with fire? Do you actually believe that? That is what this biblical writer said, but he was incorrect. This writer did not have the understanding of another prophet who said, "What does the Lord require of you but to do justice, love mercy, and walk humbly with God?"

When we read the truth, we have to sit in judgment of our own conclusion. When I know I am right, I am on dangerous ground. Try it in your own family. If you are sure of the decisions you make as a parent, you may tell your child emphatically, "I know I am right," and that may be true. But if that is your consistent attitude, do you realize what can happen? You can lose your child. You and I are never so vulnerable as when we are positive we are right.

On occasion, I think we try to please God by being sure we worship in the proper way. We want to belong to the right church or denomination; we think that is pleasing to God. Quite obviously, I believe worship is important; my life has been spent in the church. I think there is significance in what we do in church, but we know that sometimes that is an effort to find out what really matters. Look at what happened to Elijah—he was so positive that people were worshipping the wrong way by offering sacrifices to Baal that he was determined to have those people eliminated. Above all else, he wanted people to worship God properly. As you know, most of the wars in the world have been fought as holy wars. Religion has been behind so much disunion. The Bible unites us on one hand and almost at the same time divides us. Religion, the one quality that ought to bring us together, can be so divisive. Unfortunately when we speak of "our religion," what we usually mean is, "Come and be like I am." That is not fair. Is that what religion means to us? We think it is pleasing to God when we worship properly, and we decide what the proper way is because we assume we understand God.

What appealed most to Elijah? Was it the altruistic idea of loving Yahweh, or was it that he wanted to be the winner? He proposed a contest, as if to say, "I want to show you where the power is. I am going to show you who God is, and if I am right, that proves how much strength I have. Build my altar and I will demonstrate what God will do."

We need to be honest with ourselves and acknowledge that we simply like to win. By itself there is nothing wrong with that; it is neutral; but it has the potential of being good or bad, destructive or constructive. If we have no interest in winning, if we don't care for ourselves, we have a problem and we may destroy ourselves. But if our only concern is winning and we are insensitive to the needs of others, we may walk over them and destroy them. It is important to assess our motives periodically. We really like to get ahead—in our country, our society, our families, and as individuals. That is not necessarily bad, unless it means that while we are winning, we destroy other people.

I heard about something that happened at a shopping center recently. A woman was looking for a parking place in a very crowded lot. She finally found a place, but just as she was maneuvering her large car into the space, a young man in a small sports car pulled in ahead of her. As he jumped out of his car and headed for a store, the woman stopped her car, got out and called to him, "Why did you do that?" He walked back to her and replied, "Because I'm young and fast." Then he turned and walked into a store. This very dignified-looking lady got back into her car and proceeded to hit his small car with her large one, time and time again. A crowd began to gather. The young man ran out of the store and called to her, "Why did you do that?" Calmly she stepped out of her car, walked over to him, and said, "You may be young and fast, but I'm old and rich." There is something of that in every last one of us. We like to win. We need some of that quality upon which to build, but if we have that and nothing more, we will not be sensitive to other people.

What kind of an attitude did Elijah have? He was trying so hard to please God that he had an altar built to show who God was. When the altar had been consumed with fire, he killed people, under the pretense of being religious. The fact that we like to win is one of the reasons why some of the atrocious, inhumane things in the world have been done by those who claim to be religious.

We need to be introspective and ask ourselves, "When I am trying to be religious and please God, what am I doing? What is happening to me? Have I changed anything basic in my life in the last few years? Do I really think I am right? And if I am right, how do I act about it? In the long run, what do I want to happen in my life? What is significant in my life?" We do not spend much time evaluating our lives. We should go off by ourselves and think for a while. Many of the people we admire the most are those who spend much of their time alone. Granted, at times that is not their choice. Yet many of the great thoughts of the world have come to us from those who, for one reason or another, were in a position in which they could do little else but reflect.

When we look through the Bible, we realize that Jesus was by himself many times; the introspection. Jesus would not let people call him "good." Elijah wanted people to know how good he was. Elijah was saying, "I am good enough, Ahab; I can tell you it is not going to rain for three years, until I give the word. Why, I am so close to God that I can dispose of the prophets of Baal. I have power. If you cross me, Ahab, you are crossing God; that's how it is." We should run that through our minds, because that is the way we can act. Jesus was not like that at all. He was put on a cross and he did not fight back, although he was not weak. He could afford to do what he did because he had the truth. When we read about Elijah, he had to speak in a loud voice because he was scared and was bluffing. Jesus could speak softly, because he knew what he was talking about. There was all the difference in the world in these two.

Basically, what is your life? Is it one of pretense, of finesse, of manipulation? Do you say, "I am so afraid of myself, O God, that I do not want to spend time alone. I really have to bear down on other people to let them know how wrong they are." Is that how our religion affects us?

Think of the utter confidence God must have in the human race to trust us with ideas. He doesn't manipulate us. He gave us minds that can think all kinds of things. Why, if we were to create something, we would want to control it. That is why we want to gain knowledge; that is why we want to achieve developments in science; that is why we want to get ahead—why we want to win. So often what we do with our accomplishments is to destroy each other. We are like Elijah.

What really pleases God? Caring for people and caring for ourselves. That is so obvious and so simple. Doesn't the Bible say that repeatedly? Sometimes it is said so obscurely that we have to lift away layer upon layer to uncover it. At other times it is quite conspicuous, like one magnificent jewel that we cannot overlook. In the mind of God, what do you think matters? How do you please him? Jesus said it succinctly—"Love God with all your heart, soul, mind, and strength." That in itself may not mean much to us; it is just a theory. But Jesus knew how to focus it when he said, "Love your neighbor as you love yourself." That is powerful!

We please God by learning to care for ourselves, not when we are isolated, but when we are in society, with humanity, caring for people. "Well done, good and faithful servant. You have been faithful over a few things and I will now make you master over many." That passage is often interpreted in terms of immortality. "In this life you have been faithful over a few things, so when you die I will give you much to be faithful over." That may be true, but it will take care of itself.

It seems to me that God is referring to the here and now. God would like to say to us, "You have been faithful over a few things here, and now you can get ready to live in this world, this life." God's need for this world is not that more of us die to become angels in heaven. God needs the thinking that was in the mind of Jesus Christ to be alive in our hearts and minds in this world, here and now. Unless that happens, every new year will become an old year, and all we will do is switch the calendar. We should change our way of looking at life. Jesus Christ taught so magnificently: "Like yourself and care for other people." Isn't that what really pleases God?

Help Where You Do Not Expect It

When we read the Bible, we bring our presuppositions with us. In the more familiar passages we not only may assume we know the ending, but also all the twists of the story. At times this can be an asset; in other instances it is a liability. What comes to your mind when you think of Mary? Many refer to her as the Mother of God. There is a church in Canada, an enormous structure of great architectural beauty, Ste. Anne de Beaupre. A bone is encased near the High Altar of that church which is said to be a part of the arm of Anne, Mary's mother. The thought is that this is part of the arm that rocked the Mother of God. I am not critical of those who refer to Mary as the Mother of God, although we do not do so in the Protestant churches. Yet we are very much aware of her significance. We know she is the mother of Jesus. With that knowledge and the implications of the other ideas about her running through our minds, we cannot imagine that a woman could have a more glorious or wonderful experience. Consequently, when we read of her troubles and heartaches we almost dismiss them as if they were not real. After all, we think, she is the most admired and loved woman in Christianity. If we could rid ourselves of our predispositions and reread her life, I wonder what woman would really want to trade places with her.

What did it actually mean to be Mary? She was a young woman who realized she was pregnant. That was a threat to her; she was frightened. How would you explain that to anyone; a virgin, who would believe her story? Joseph was on the verge of leaving her, but instead they went to Bethlehem together. If Joseph had nothing to do with her predicament, why did they go to Bethlehem? After all, it was Joseph who was of the house and lineage of David from which the Messiah was expected to come.

So often, in the Old Testament, the men were portrayed as doing the "begetting," and often the women were omitted. It is almost as if children were born to the men. When we reach the New Testament, the women are allowed to do it. I thought it took two. Is that embarrassing? Does that somehow shock us? Are we so fragile that we cannot recognize the beauty of what is? The birth of Jesus is saying to all of us that life is sacred, that God is within us. Mary was young, she was pregnant, and she was frightened. She and Joseph went to Bethlehem, and Jesus was born in a stable because there was no room for them in the inn. Shortly after that, they fled into Egypt.

Later they returned, and we read about them again when Jesus was about twelve years old. They had gone to Jerusalem to celebrate the Passover, and for two or three days Jesus was lost in the temple. On their way home, they realized that they did not know where he was. Joseph thought he was with Mary, and

Mary thought he was with Joseph, since the women and men traveled in separate groups. This was done for their protection. A number of the women would be sent on ahead with some men, and the other men would follow behind; then in the evening they would meet as families. The next day they would regroup to continue their journey.

We also read about Mary and Jesus when he was about thirty years old. One day he spoke in the synagogue in Nazareth, and he was run out of the city. That was the beginning of his public ministry; when he preached his first sermon, we might say. When he began his itinerant ministry, Mary did not want him to go. I'm on her side; Mary knew her son. She probably knew his mind better than anyone besides Jesus himself. She knew he was going to teach with clarity about mercy, kindness, and love—fragile things that were going against the status quo, the might. His ideas would almost appear naïve. She also knew that one of two things would happen—either people would have to change, which was very unlikely, or Jesus would be hurt.

So, with her other children, Mary went to the house where Jesus was and sent in word that his mother and his brothers and sister were outside. His reply, I think, is translated poorly. We don't know exactly what Jesus said, of course. When you read it in a very precise, blunt way he is supposed to have said, "Who is my mother; who are my brothers and sisters?" We should look at his response with some understanding of the direction his life was taking. Then he answered

49

his own question: "Those who do the will of my father." That implies, "Mary is my mother if she does God's will." Doesn't that sound religious? I doubt he said it like that at all.

Mary was saying to Jesus, "I'm out here, Jesus; don't take the risk; come back home. What do you expect to accomplish? Who do you think will believe you, or even listen to you? Do you really expect people to believe that love matters? If you try to change the fabric of society, they will annihilate you. Come back home." And Jesus, I think, was telling Mary, "I understand, but you must realize that you have brought me to this point; your life has been risky. Look at the trouble I have caused you from the very moment you knew I was to be born. Your whole life has been filled with uncertainties—you went to Bethlehem, where you had no place to spend the night except in a stable; you had to flee into Egypt because of me; you came back home, and one day you lost me and you were worried. But, during all that time you were teaching me to take risks. And now, are you asking me to play it safe? If I came home and lived as you ask, I would be discrediting what your life has stood for; you have taken risks for me, haven't you? And now that is exactly what I must do." This, it seems to me, is really a completion of what Mary was. But the love of a mother would say, "Don't do it."

The last time we read about Mary, Jesus is hanging on the cross and says very clearly to her, "Behold, your son. I will not be here, so this is your son now, and he will take care of you." To one of his disciples, he said,

"This is your mother; take her home; don't keep her here any longer." There is help where you do not expect to find it. Wouldn't you have thought that God would have taken care of Mary? "God, if you are in this at all, take care of the person you have called." That seems fair, does it not? It seems to me that that is the very least we could expect.

When we look at our own lives, we realize that many times we have been hurt when we did not expect to be hurt, by someone we did not expect to hurt us. When that occurs, it is painful, and when it happens to a teenager or to a child, it is devastating. If you are a teenager and you love someone who is very close to you and that person hurts you, you almost try to block it out of your mind. You try to deny it, because it is too painful. If we live long enough, I suppose everyone of us will have been hurt by someone we did not expect to hurt us. We can recall many instances of this in our own lives, and there are numerous illustrations of it in the Bible.

In the Old Testament there was a time when David, as a young boy, was brought to the court of King Saul. Saul had frequent headaches, and when David played his harp, Saul was soothed and felt better. They were friends, and for a while Saul looked upon David almost as a son. Then, over a period of time, Saul became jealous of David. One day, when David had returned from the battlefield, Saul heard women singing in the streets, "Saul has killed his thousands, but David has killed his tens of thousands," and this was more than Saul could take. Jealousy overwhelmed him, and he decided that David was his enemy. You know the story—Saul tried many times to kill David or to have him killed. Who would have thought it? You might say, "Why, Saul, David is your backer; you should know that you don't have a better friend than David." On several occasions, David had a chance to kill Saul, but he did not. Instead, he left some token behind to say, "I could have taken your life, but I am your friend and I didn't do it."

Just as we may be hurt by someone we did not expect to hurt us, there are times when we are helped by someone we did not expect to help us. That has happened to me in the church. No doubt anyone who works in a charitable organization has had similar experiences, and I expect most of you have found this to be true in your own businesses, in your own lives. There have been occasions when I would work hard in an organization to accomplish something that I thought would be of value. At such times there were certain people I knew I could depend upon; but they didn't carry through. I would find myself at a loss, thinking, "What do I do now?" And then one person, or a group of people, unexpectedly helped when help was so desperately needed.

If we want help in life, and if I tell you that it is possible to get help where we least expect it, we must consider what kind of help we need. What do we consider problems? On a world basis, hunger is a problem; trying to find peace is a problem.

In terms of international affairs, scarcely a new idea has been advanced in the last two thousand years.

Jesus came with a refreshing idea, but we haven't taken it seriously; we have negated it. Do you realize that our thinking hasn't changed much for hundreds, perhaps thousands of years? We can destroy more people more quickly, but what is original about that? The big muscle? The strong arm? The alternative is risky, isn't it, but what could be more perilous than getting ready for another war? I am not naïvely advocating pacifism, but do we ever think in terms of, "O God, here is our problem; how are we going to solve it?" We think the biblical longing for peace on earth is a poetic idea and a marvelous theme to sing about. In actuality, it is a necessary idea. It seems to me that we face two choices—either we learn to live together in this world or we eradicate those who oppose us, destroying our world at the same time.

There was a time when a preacher would speak for getting converted so that when we died we would be with God. Today we have to say, "Be converted so that you can live in this world." Unless we are converted to the idea of a loving God, our future on this planet looks bleak. What are the problems? Surely world peace is one. Inflation is another. We realize that inflation has almost overcome us, but how should we handle it? Should we simply think in terms of our own personal problems? Today we are so interrelated that if one country goes under, it affects the rest of the world. It is much like a large business failing—there is a domino effect. The bank is affected, and the bank affects other organizations. This can go only so far before we all are involved.

Thomas Jefferson was an extraordinary thinker. I think we ought to reread some of his ideas. He advocated a new constitution approximately every twenty-five years. Think of that recommendation from a man who labored so diligently over the one we have! He also suggested that we erase the national debt every twenty years, because we have no moral right to pass the debt we have accumulated to the next generation. Although he did not deal with ecology, that philosophy might be applied to ecology as well. What right do we have to pollute our world and pass the results of that pollution on to the next generation? How much can we take for ourselves and misuse, then merely apologize to those who come after us? Greed can destroy us. As long as we simply must have more of everything, how can we expect to be converted? Do we say, "O God, save me so that when I die I can go to heaven?" Is that conversion?

Mary risked her life repeatedly. But we say, "O Jesus, I have come to you and I want to be saved. Don't ask me to risk anything. Don't ask me to accept a new idea or to have to adjust. I want you to take care of me." In this day and time, we cannot be secure trying to take care of ourselves unless we find some ways of making other people secure as well. Therefore, we face a multitude of problems nationally, internationally, and personally.

Viewing the development of our society, it is strange to me that today a handful of people can create a problem, but a handful of people cannot solve it. We read about a small country where a few people with an atomic bomb can hold the rest of the world hostage. Some novels have been written about such an idea; several people can threaten the rest of the world or start another war or help to end our society. Isn't that odd? We would assume that if a handful of people could cause the problem, then a handful of people could find the solution, but it doesn't work that way. It takes a large number of people to solve the problem. It is the way we think, the way we are. Do we think in terms of goodwill, really? Have the ideas that Jesus preached made an appreciable difference in our lives?

It seems to me that if we want to make an attempt to solve problems, the place to begin is within our own lives. We have more strength and resources than we realize. That should not make us egotists or megalomaniacs; that is just a truth we need to recognize.

As individuals we cannot have much of an impact on world affairs, or national affairs, but let's start where we are. Begin with yourself, with whatever problems you deal with day by day. Jesus spoke to this when he said, "The kingdom of God is within you." In other words, we have resources within our own lives that are powerful. Think of what we are capable of doing. Jesus' words should encourage us; they tell us a lot about ourselves, and one thing we must realize is that other people do not control us. Our fate is not predetermined. To a great extent, we can choose the thoughts we will think, what we will be, and the kinds of feelings we will have. Of course, we are not in charge of our whole lives. We are not the masters of our souls; we should not want to be. But we do have resources within our lives that are almost unlimited. We should start with those. When we deal with the idea of finding help, let's start within our own lives.

A friend told me about a church in another city that was completely renovated sometime ago. What had been the chapel was relocated in another part of the building and turned into a parlor. In decorating the parlor, a wallpaper was chosen that had large flowers, black and white and brown and white. When you walked into the room, the flowered wallpaper was the first thing that caught your attention. After the redecoration was finished, an open house was held. A woman visitor walked into the parlor and exclaimed, "I don't like it! I wonder what a bride will think when she walks into this room!" A woman standing beside her was a member of that church and she said, "I was on the decorating committee." Without a moment's hesitation, the visitor remarked, "They outvoted you, didn't they?"

That is about as alert as one can be. I'm sure there are times when each of us wishes he could think that quickly. Remember, there are times when we have dynamic resources within us. We tend to forget that. We look at life with its manifold problems and think, "O God, what can I do? I'm almost helpless; it's hopeless." That is not true.

We think we get help when we directly receive what we want; that is not so. We erroneously assume that the giving primarily benefits the recipient, when in reality the giving helps the one who has given.

Sit down and reflect for a while on the things you remember about your own life. Other people have done things for you that you have taken for granted; and you have done things for other people. But, what really brings you happiness? Isn't it the time when you pushed yourself a little farther than you normally would—when you were kinder, more generous, more loving? You know what matters to you—it is when you are a giving person.

We are taught to be go-getters. Is that the kind of nation we want? What if every country in the world were only a sponge? What if individuals were like that? We brag about someone who gets ahead. What does it mean to us for people to have gotten ahead a hundred years ago? What do you think the world really needs? To find help where you do not expect it, I think we must learn to be giving, sharing people.

Individuals can donate to various charitable organizations, but suppose you do not have any money to give? Money isn't required to be generous and kind—give yourself. Stop sometime and make yourself do something for someone else. However, when you do so, be aware that the person may not be especially responsive to you; someone's response is not important. You have probably reached out to a number of people who didn't respond. That is not the issue. If you want your life to have more meaning, I think I can promise you something that will work—become a giving person. Suppose you do it for selfish reasons. Does that matter? There is nothing wrong with that. Is any motive or act totally pure? Suppose I preach for a selfish reason. Is that of paramount importance? Are you going to wait until your mind is completely pure before you do something? We need help, and this is the place to start. Give! Only in giving can we understand what it is to receive. If we have the joy of giving, one day someone will give us something and we can say, "Perhaps now I understand." Mary was giving throughout her entire life, according to the scriptures.

In the final analysis, we really get help where we do not expect it when we go back to where we were hurt. If you hurt someone or someone has hurt you, go back to that relationship. The person may not forgive you; that is not the point, you tried. Perhaps you have been embarrassed and you have tried to put that humiliation out of your mind; you would like to forget it. You cannot stand it; it threatens you and you feel awkward about it. I am not recommending that you reopen the wound and be hurt again; not at all. But look at it; recognize it. You need not be afraid any longer. Don't be frightened of your past. Maybe you have been a fool; perhaps you have done stupid, ridiculous things. That is of no consequence. If you really want to grow up and have something of significance in your life, here is where you may find help: go back to where you were hurt.

Now, join me as I remember a time years ago when I had an experience that affected me then and will affect me for the rest of my life. A friend of mine, one of the kindest men I have ever known, drove into a service station, as he had done many times before. He went inside and saw a man he knew very well, who was quite drunk. The man began to curse my friend and say all sorts of embarrassing things to him. My friend tried to get away, but the other man followed him to his car and continued to swear at him. Finally, my friend turned and pushed him slightly. The man staggered and fell. As he did so, he hit his head on the concrete and died instantly.

The news spread rapidly in this small town where we all knew one another. Almost as soon as I heard about it, my friend called me to his home to be with him and, of course, I went. As we sat together he said, "Barry, I don't know why I did that. Why didn't I just let him say whatever he wanted to say? I would never have hurt that man. Why did I shove him?" After a while he said, "You know what I have to do. I must go and see his wife." He asked me to go with him. I had planned to visit her anyway, because she was a friend of mine too. In a few short hours that town had become divided. We had all been friends, but now there was obvious, heavy tension in the air.

I remember so many details of the widow's house as we approached it that night; what the rooms looked like, the front porch, people standing outside. When we walked up, no one really spoke to us, although normally they would have. We entered the living room and my friend said, "I've come to see her; I must see her." Someone went to the back of the house to speak to her. After a brief wait, a man returned and said,

"She wants to see you." He showed us into a bedroom where an older lady sat in a rocking chair. Driving to the house, both of us had wondered what my friend would say, but he never had a chance to say very much; I don't believe I remember a word that he said. As soon as he walked into that bedroom, that lovely lady said, "Honey, I have known you since you were a little boy; don't you know that I realize you would not have done this for anything in the world?" And she hugged him. Immediately, the town began to be healed. We do get strength and help when we go back to where we were hurt.

Now, where is Mary? Her son, about thirty-three years old, is dying on a cross; and where is she? Standing by the cross. When Jesus began his ministry, she said, "Don't do it; come back home." But he continued; he lived and taught so well and with such lucidity that the world had to do one of two things: either follow him or try to get rid of him. But Mary was there. And that is where she found her healing. Think of what he said to her. To one of his disciples, he said, "Now she is your mother." And to her, he said, "This is your son." She found her healing—where she was being hurt. Jesus had hurt her, but now she is being helped, healed. Almost every pain Mary experienced was because of Jesus. But it was worth it, was it not?

The Danger
of Purity

All of us like purity. We appreciate it in music—a singer who has perfect pitch, an orchestra whose instruments blend in total harmony. We dislike noise, cacophony. Purity in literature also appeals to us—words that flow together in a rhythm that draws us into the author's meaning. We like to see ideas presented so ingeniously that what is implied is more conspicuous than what is written.

We desire—in fact we almost demand—a certain purity with respect to the arts, with respect to life, and especially with respect to religion. Certainly we want our religion to be pure. We do value purity. Therefore, perhaps it's not unusual that when you come right down to it, you and I would like to be pure.

It has often been said, "There was only one perfect life and that was Jesus of Nazareth." We glibly repeat that, yet often we do not even know what we are talking about. A perfect life? Does that make a difference? Do you think that Jesus had to be perfect to be our Savior? What did the so-called "good people" who loved purity say about him? They said, "He is a winebibber and a glutton. He eats with the wrong people. He does not even do the right thing at the proper time—he heals on the wrong day. It is the Sabbath, and look what he has done."

Don't you suppose Jesus was concerned about goodness and purity? Of course he was, but purity alone can be devastating. What will prevent America from becoming a sick, overly zealous religious country if we continue to say, "O God, give us a pure understanding of the Bible, give us the pure word, God. We want to know you; and by all means, we want you on our side, God. We want to win!" Jesus' life was not like that at all.

Hitler was a purist; he envisioned a pure race. Remember what he wanted, what he planned for. The sicker you become, the more determined you may be that you are infallible. You are deaf to the truth about yourself, you are unable to recognize your weaknesses. You believe you cannot err in any respect. If you become sick enough, you may be convinced that you are completely right and see yourself as God's gift to the universe, as Hitler did.

Parochial minds tried to do that with Jesus, they tried to make him a figure of absolute purity, but he did not accept that. The church in his time could not dispose of Jesus by crucifying him. We have gotten rid of him today in a far more effective way—by bragging on him, while failing to listen to him.

The desire to be pure can destroy relationships. How can anyone be honest with you? Visualize a situation in dealing with your children. You, as the parent, are sure you are right. You have been forgiven for whatever sins you may have committed, and you would not think of ever doing anything wrong again. You belong to God; you are pure. Then one day your child comes to you in a moment of despair and tries to talk with you openly and honestly about a problem he or she is facing. Suppose that problem is something threatening involving a moral situation that the child knows you will call immoral. How can that child tell you where he hurts? The desire for purity can be destructive. It can make us lie; it can destroy us.

However, if we have creative goodness in our lives, there is really no way that purity can be our primary concern. We want to be good, to be responsible; but if our goodness is to be creative, we will have to make choices.

One day Jesus called two men to be his disciples. He called twelve, of course, but I refer to the day he called the sons of Zebedee, James and John. They were in a boat with their father, mending their nets, when Jesus said, "Come and follow me." And the Bible says, "And they left their father, Zebedee, in the boat working on the nets, and they went with Jesus." I suppose Zebedee wished he had been called, too, instead of being left with nets to mend. Imagine his going home and telling his wife, "We lost our sons. They followed an itinerant preacher down the road."

What was Jesus about to teach James and John? He was going to tell them how to be good. What does it take to be good? Concern for people. He was going to teach them to be sensitive to the needs of others. We might stop Jesus a few feet away and ask, "Jesus, if that is the case, why didn't you let them stay and work with their father for awhile? Couldn't he have used some help?" It is strange, but we can't be totally pure if we are creatively good. We have to make some hard choices. For instance, when we help one person, we may hurt another. We cannot give to one cause without neglecting something else. We cannot select unless we reject. Three of the disciples that Jesus called to be with him were especially close to him, but what about the other nine? If we are creatively good, we are no longer totally pure, because life involves us in contradictions.

Despite this, in an effort to seem pure we talk about witnessing for God and for Christ, when we are actually witnessing for ourselves. We want those around us to know how good we are. If I am witnessing to you about God or Christ, and I become angry when you disagree with me, what is it that makes me angry? Surely it is not that you do not understand God or Christ; you may understand better than I do. Chances are I am threatened because you disagree with me. So often we witness for ourselves, rather than for God or Christ.

One day some people turned to Jesus and asked, "By what authority are you doing these things?" And he replied, "I want to ask you a question. Answer me and I will tell you by what authority I do these things. John the Baptist, was he of God or of man?" They went off to one side and began to discuss his question among themselves. They reasoned, "If we say he is of man, then the followers of John the Baptist—and there are many of them standing around here—will turn on us." So they returned to Jesus and said, "We cannot answer your question." And Jesus said, "Neither will I answer your question."

Surely we think Jesus was religious, but compare the way Jesus responded to his questioners to the way we would respond. Suppose we had been in Jesus' place that day, doing good works, when someone asked, "By what authority are you doing this?" Oh, we wouldn't have hesitated to answer, "God's authority! God has given it to me." What does that reply actually disclose about us? It reveals that our response is, in effect, "I want you to know how good I am, how great I am. Look at what God is doing through me. But don't give me the credit, give it to God." We shouldn't blame what we have done on God. He has enough problems as it is; dealing with us is a full-time job.

Jesus was intelligent—he stood there and said to them, "I'm not going to tell you. Why don't you look at what I am doing?" For whom was he witnessing? He was witnessing for God by asking a question; he was witnessing for God by remaining silent. But look at us! We want to run out and lay our message on the world, and we claim to witness for God when we do it.

Needless to say, witnessing is important, but it can be neurotic. Let's be candid with ourselves. If we really love God, other people, and ourselves, we need not run around shouting about it; we don't have to impress others.

Jesus was so aware of God's presence that he could be quiet. He was asked, "Tell me, Jesus, by what authority do you do this?" What do you think a religious person living today would have said? His probable reply would be, "Thank God! This is my chance. God gave me the authority!" Who is that person witnessing for? Yet Jesus stood there, very much aware of God, of his own identity, and of people. He didn't have to say anything, only ask a question. Jesus liked purity. But more than purity, he was concerned with reality, responsibility, beauty, and truth.

Our desire to be pure includes several areas that are important to us. One of them is our nation; we want a pure country. In America we see ourselves almost as the new Jerusalem, believing that God brought our country into existence. That is what we claim and evidently believe, due to some form of exaggerated patriotism. We should thank God for our country, but America is not really God's gift to the world. What kind of God would choose only one group of people?

The Jew has seen himself as chosen of God, and the Bible says that God chose the Jew. However, the Jew wrote the book. Read what some Irish have to say about the Catholics. When you write the rules and the outcome, you can be predominant. Of course God can work with the Jew, and the Jew has made a unique contribution, a necessary contribution, but it has evolved through a long process of growth. The Jew, at his best, realizes he is a significant part of humanity, but that he is neither better nor above other members of the human race. And so it is with America.

We talk about Columbus discovering America—what do you suppose the Indians were doing for so many years? Were they waiting here for Columbus to discover them? In fact, he never reached America at all. He wasn't really sure where he was.

The discovery of a ten-thousand-year-old skeleton found near Austin, Texas, was made public a short while ago. Ten thousand years old? That was a long time to wait for Columbus, wasn't it? But, of course, we wrote our history books. According to our chronicles we discovered this land and made it European. Our interpretation is that the white race did it. I can just see God sitting in heaven thinking, "I will be so glad when Columbus finally discovers America and we can get this going properly!" Do you think the Indians, who had been here all along, were just waiting for our great discovery?

Not only do we want to have a pure country, but we also want a pure religion. Sometime ago I heard that the religious people in America can be divided into two groups. One group says, "I believe in the Bible," and the other segment says, "I believe it more than you do." That describes us rather accurately. We are determined to be more religious than any other people in the history of the planet Earth.

In addition, we want a pure family. It is normal to be proud of your family, to feel joy regarding your relatives. Some of us have family members who diligently trace their ancestry. We would like to think that all of our ancestors graduated from the appropriate schools, held responsible positions, and were trustworthy citizens, but that is not necessarily true. When we allow ourselves to think that way, we are deceiving ourselves.

Sometime ago I was talking with a lawyer. I asked him to tell me about the most interesting case he had ever handled. "Actually," he said, "the most interesting case I ever had I did not take." An attorney in another part of the state had called and asked to consult with him. A man had died without leaving a will, and the man's common-law wife wanted to claim her share of his estate. The attorney asked my friend to help him with the case.

My lawyer friend said he believed they could win and agreed to join him. But he reconsidered when the other lawyer admitted there were ramifications—the man was white, the woman black. "That does complicate matters," my friend told him. "As a matter of fact, there is no way we can win because Texas law prohibits mixed marriages between whites and blacks. Even if they are married in conventional ceremonies, it is not recognized as legal. Surely a common-law marriage wouldn't be recognized, so this widow has no legal claim and there isn't any way in the world she can win." As far as he was concerned, that was the end of it.

About two years later, my friend was in Houston for a convention and saw a limousine drive up to the hotel; the other lawyer got out of it. My friend admired the limousine, thinking it might have been rented, but the man told him it was his own car. "I got this from the case I called you about—you remember, the one you told me I couldn't win because it involved a common-law marriage between a white and a black. Well, after I talked to you, I thought more about her contention and decided to pursue it further. I thought about it and decided that she wasn't black, but a full-blooded Cherokee Indian, and we won!"

Doesn't that kind of represent where we are? We think, "Pure, O God, always pure." Every last one of us wants purity, yet none of us is really pure. We want so much to have a pure family, and we are embarrassed when a member of our family does something of which we do not approve. We would like to hide whatever has been done because it threatens and frightens us.

Furthermore, we want to be pure in our profession. You would not want a minister to come into the pulpit without praying before he spoke. But wouldn't you be uncomfortable if my overriding prayer was, "O God make our church stronger than any other; let us get more members than any other congregation in the city"? It would be inexcusable if I felt that way. But suppose that were true and we experienced enormous growth, then I could come before you and say, "God must be blessing us because we are growing faster than everybody else. God is on our side, so we must be right." In that case, to what do we pay tribute—God or success?

You see, we want to do well in every area of our lives, but too often we seem to be anxious to get God on our side so we can win big.

In contrast to our manipulative efforts, how did Jesus treat God? Even when pressed, when his back was against the wall, he didn't use God to win. He never won, but he was right. He was honest; he was true; he was loving. Some people said Jesus wasn't pure, but he was better than pure—he was real. Something truly pure frightens us away; we are afraid to get near it.

Quite frankly, I do not believe God calls us to be pure. God calls us to be honest, to be authentic. But most of all, God calls us to be ourselves. If we do that, goodness will be a by-product of our lives; but if our main goal is to be pure and to be right, we can become religious fanatics and be dangerous to ourselves and to others.

We need to realize that no matter how much we may desire purity, we are not pure. Being converted and baptized does not make us pure. The result of conversion should be to make us aware of the whole self—our contradictions, our generosity, our selfishness, our profound thoughts and our petty thoughts—the convergence of our whole being. We are not pure. We never have been and we never will be. Thank God that we are not, for that is our hope. As long as we know we haven't achieved perfection, there is still something to work toward. Strive as we may, we will never be pure. As human beings we need all the help we can get.

And where do we find this help? It is the grace of God, not any effort of ours, that saves us for heaven and this life as well. So often we leave the impression that we save ourselves. We seem to imply that we can save ourselves by a pure understanding of God, by a right comprehension of the Bible, by having the right faith. We want others to think we have worked it all out ourselves, when it is God's grace that actually saves us. Think what could happen to us if we had to be responsible for our own salvation. Suppose I claim to be witnessing for God through Christ when I say, "I want you to know what I have done; I have been converted. Before this happened to me my life was lost, but now that I have found Christ, see how well I am doing." As you can see, actually I would be witnessing for myself.

Our desire for purity is not only futile but uncalled for, because relationships are what really matter in life, not principles. Principles are important, of course, but they are not the focal point of Christianity. A relationship is primary in Christianity and that is what Jesus was offering. We tend to think that the main difference between the early church and the Jewish church centered on whether or not Jesus Christ was the Savior. That is a misconception. The significant difference was whether to follow a set of principles, rules, or to follow a relationship. This is biblically sound.

Now the Christians have missed the point just as much as the Jews did, so this is not to say the Jew was wrong and the Christian right. The real issue here is, "Are you going to follow principles and rules, though they are important in their place, or are you going to follow relationships?" As a good Jew, Jesus was concerned about the Sabbath, but to him people took precedence over the Sabbath. He was concerned about worship, but people were of greater consequence. It is relationship that truly matters.

A recent movie is about an actor who could not find a job as a man, so he dressed himself as a woman and was hired for a role. While he was masquerading as a woman, he fell in love with a woman who also was a member of the cast. Because she came to know him as her best friend, "Dorothy," he faced an unusual problem. He could not let her know he was in love with her, because he was living and playing the role of a woman. Later, when he finally revealed the truth to her, she felt tricked and didn't want to have anything to do with him. Then he was hurt because he loved her very much, but he didn't know how they could get together.

One day he waited outside the studio until she came out and then followed her. Before crossing a street, she hesitated just long enough for him to ask, "May I call you?" She turned around and they began to talk. As she looked at him she said, "I miss Dorothy." "She is still here," he replied. I like that line. There was a heterosexual man, saying to the woman he loves, "She is still here. Whatever you liked in me earlier, regardless of how I was dressed, that is still me. I am a person." (I think Paul was right: "When love is in your heart you are not slave or free, man or woman; you are you; you are who you are.") And then he looked at her and said, "When I was with you, I was more a man, as a woman, than I was a man with other women." That

76

caught her attention and she asked, "If I come back to see you, will you let me have that little yellow dress?" And he answered, "No, you'd ruin it." Then they joined hands and walked down the sidewalk, almost bouncing along. The fade-out music played and they hugged each other.

What did those two people really want? They wanted what you truly want—a relationship. Principles matter, of course. You would like to be pure in some respects. You want to do well, even excel; you would like to know more than you can ever know. You would like to let your life blossom and grow. You want to be religious. You want to succeed in your profession. You want to be proud of yourself, your family, your country. But what do you want most of all? Jesus was so aware. He refused to fall into the purity trap. He refused to let people fall into the goodness trap. He even refused to let people call him "good." But he chose to follow truth and growth; the relationship.

One day some people said to Jesus, "I want to ask you a question: by what authority are you doing these things?" That would have been a perfect opportunity for him to be pure and say, "God gave me the authority." But he was so internally secure that he did not have to bluff externally, and he replied, "Let me ask you a question and if you answer it, I will answer your question—was John the Baptist of God or of man?" They pondered that for a little while, then they came back to Jesus and said, "We do not know." And

Jesus told them, "Then I will not answer your question." That is reality; that is playing both sides of the record. It is an example of being aware of your goodness and your vulnerability, your strength and your weakness, your purity and impurity. I think that is what God needs from his people.

Hopefully you will go ahead and become converted to God through Christ, but please, in the name of common sense and everything worthwhile, never let your conversion make you into a pompous, religious fanatic. If you do, as absurd as it may sound, you will be trying to be more religious than Jesus ever dared to be. Religion at its best always is involved with reality and with life.

The War
of the
Gods

What really makes one religion better than another? As Christians, can we assume that we have all the truth or that God prefers us to everyone else? Is God actually at war against other gods or varying concepts of God? Jesus once counseled, "If they are not against us, they are for us." He was a thinker. "Know the truth and the truth will make you free."

With the above as a preface to our thoughts, let us go back to the time of Paul's visit to Athens. He had been converted several years earlier, and possessed a fervor, a profound devotion. He went to Athens, to Mars' Hill, where he was going to preach to the Athenians. Regrettably for Paul, he tackled them on their own territory. They were philosophical; they could handle an idea. To this day they have a corner on the market, as far as philosophy is concerned. Not only that, if I had been a Greek, Paul would have lost me at the beginning, because he said, "I notice that you are very superstitious." No one wants their religion called superstition. In reality, what is myth and what is faith? By our definition, our religion always seems to be faith and someone else's is myth. Nonetheless, Paul said, "I notice that you are very superstitious, because as I walked along I saw your magnificent temples and one bore the inscription 'to an unknown god.' " Paul's tactlessness doesn't diminish as he continues, "That is the one I want to discuss with you, 'the unknown god,' the one you worship in your ignorance. I want to share my intelligence with you."

Would that approach win anyone over? The Athenians did not debate with Paul; they ignored him. He failed. No wonder! His thesis was, "I want you to believe in God, the God that created everything—the heavens, the earth, and all." They could handle that easily. That was no problem for the Greeks who thought in terms of the here, the hereafter, the now, the out there. They were fully cognizant of their gods; they created myths about their gods and added to them; their myths grew with the telling. Paul had said, "I want to talk with you about the God that created the heavens and the earth. Then I want to tell you about his son, our Lord and Savior, who was crucified, dead, and buried, and was raised from the dead." The Greeks were not swayed by that.

From the Christian point of view, we want to admonish them, "They should have believed Paul; he offered them Jesus and they did not accept him. They were so carried away with their myths, they could not accept the great Christian faith!" May I ask why they should have? Paul said, "Here is one man who was crucified, dead, and buried, and raised from the dead." The Greeks had far more impressive stories telling them that Zeus could give birth to other gods just out of his head. They had fantasies and myths galore; why should hearing about one man who was crucified, dead, and buried, and then arose and walked, make an impression on them? They could beat that story, hands down.

The one ingredient Paul did not deal with was the idea of ethics. Why not? Perhaps I am completely off base, but I strongly suspect my assumption is correct—Paul did not deal with ethics at this time because, as we know, Paul never knew Jesus personally, never studied with him. That is fine; we are glad that he didn't because from Paul we learn how we can relate to Jesus. Who would have taught him about Jesus? Remember, Paul was converted and about three years later he went back to Jerusalem, remaining there for some two weeks. Simon Peter didn't teach Paul about Jesus because they didn't get along very well. They were never that close. Paul was deeply dedicated to Jesus; he was converted to Jesus. We should not overlook either aspect of Paul's life. But what about the teachings of Jesus? Suppose you fall in love with mathematics—does it naturally follow that you know how to solve mathematical problems?

Perhaps Paul was not very well informed about what Jesus taught when he spoke at Mars' Hill. "If my kingdom were of this world, then my soldiers would fight," Jesus said, "but my kingdom is not of this world." Jesus asked us to pray that the kingdom of God would come into this world. He also said, "If I thought as you thought, I would fight, too, but I don't think as you think. I wish you thought as I do. . . . Blessed are the merciful. . . . Blessed are you when

you forgive people who despise you and use you. . . .
Blessed are you when you are hungry and thirsty for
righteousness. . . . Blessed are you when you are pure
enough in heart so that you are not encumbered by
yourself and you can think. . . . Know the truth and
the truth will make you free." These are all ethical
ideas, but Paul did not mention principles on Mars
Hill. Instead he dealt with the one thing that held so
much meaning for him—the resurrection of Jesus.
That has validity, of course. But why didn't Paul move
into the realm of ethics, the one area about which the
Greeks had little to say?

To the Greeks, Zeus was the most significant god;
their supreme god. Beneath Zeus were many lesser
gods; the Greeks created a god to cover every
contingency. If the sea was rough—Poseidon caused
it. Since everything that happened was involved with
a god, they created marvelous stories, sometimes
macabre ones concerning their gods.

Zeus, of course, was the most powerful. He could do
almost everything he wanted to do, but he could not
always have his way. To the Greek mind, the gods had
fun. They were involved in intrigue; they were
involved in love and sexual liaisons; they were
involved in all sorts of fascinating machinations. The
Greeks didn't need television or much external
stimulation; they just sat down and talked about their
gods, and there was all the excitement imaginable.

According to one of their myths, Zeus designated
the responsibility of caring for all the animals on
earth to Prometheus and his brother, Epimetheus.

Epimetheus became carried away with his assignment, taking such good care of the animals that there were no reserves, no talents left for the human race. This saddened Prometheus. He knew the animals were protected during the cold—their hair grew thicker; they could eat grass; they were cared for by nature. But look at people, he thought, no one cares for them. They are cold and they don't have fire. So, the myth tells us that Prometheus went to heaven and stole fire and brought it to the human race. This so enraged Zeus, the powerful god of all gods, that he had Prometheus chained to a rocky peak. Once each day a vulture came and tore at Prometheus' liver, trying to kill him. He might have died, but every night his liver healed and grew back. The vulture returned each day; this continued for thousands and thousands of years.

Does that story sound familiar? "If you don't believe in God, in Yahweh, he can send you to hell. Hellfire and brimstone! When you die you are going to stand before God, and if you don't believe in God as you should, you go to hell." We may wonder what "believe in God as you should" means. Some say it means, "Believe in Jesus Christ as Lord and Savior." What does that say to the Jew? The response to that question has been, "Well, room will be made for the Jew, too." We are not really sure what "believe in God as you should" signifies, but if we don't have it right, if we don't have faith, if we are not Christians, if we are not religious, we are told we will go to hell, where we will burn forever and ever and ever.

While we can be consigned to eternal hell, a Greek myth tells us that Prometheus was chained to a rock for thousands and thousands of years because he disobeyed Zeus. Prometheus was trying to bring fire to people, but Zeus didn't tell him to do that and Zeus is god. Where are the ethics in this story? Supposedly, Prometheus remained bound to the peak until Hercules freed him. And neither the punishment nor the passage of time assuaged Zeus' anger. He was still so incensed that he decided punishment for the friend of man was not enough; he would also punish mankind as well—by creating an object that all men would desire, thereby causing more problems than they could handle. He called in some of the lesser gods and told them what he wanted. Hephaestus created Pandora. The legend of Pandora and her box is a familiar one.

Created in the image of a shy maiden, Pandora was lovely to look upon. Aphrodite gave her beauty, Hermes gave her flattery and the ability to be cunning, Athena gave her knowledge of the arts. The gods also gave her a box which they warned her never to open. She came to Prometheus' brother, Epimetheus, and presented herself. Prometheus mistrusted this gift of the gods and cautioned his brother not to have anything to do with her. But she was so attractive that Epimetheus could not resist her. Despite the warnings, he accepted her. Finally, one day, Pandora was carrying her box and she couldn't resist any longer; her curiosity got the best of her. She lifted the lid of the box, just for a moment, and out flew all of the sins, the vices, the innumerable diseases, and troubles which would continue to afflict the world. Pandora clapped the lid down, but it was too late. Only one element remained in the box—hope.

Isn't that an interesting story? It is easy to dismiss it as a myth, but how did the Greeks develop such a tale? From the standpoint of theology, we use the phrase empirical learning—observation. The Greeks looked at life and asked, "Where did all the vices come from? The evil, the diseases?" They devised a story to answer their questions, saying, "These things were given to us because we disobeyed Zeus."

We are familiar with comparable stories. According to the Book of Genesis, why does a man have to work hard? Why does a woman suffer when she gives birth to a child? Hundreds and hundreds of years ago, these questions must have been asked. People probably thought, "It is hard to make a living; sometimes the soil is so thin. If you have animals, you have to keep moving your herd. You have children, and before you know it, there is another mouth to feed. Why does that happen?" And so the answer began to evolve: "I know why it happens—because our forefathers sinned against Yahweh." They wondered what their fore-bears had done to anger Yahweh, and they came up with an answer: "They broke his law; they ate of the tree of knowledge; they wanted to be gods. We deserve what we are getting. So, a man will always have to work hard and a woman will bear children in pain."

And then Jesus came, teaching. He taught with clarity; he did not speak as other people. He made sense. Jesus did not always take a stand on the side of the establishment. He wrapped his arms around people in trouble, but he did not excuse our sins and weaknesses by saying, "Cheer up, it's all right. It will come out in the wash!" The judgment was in love, and the love was in judgment; thus there is hope. Because of that, precisely at our weakest points, we feel we may become stronger. Someone asked Jesus, "What is the most important thing in life? What is the greatest commandment?" His response was not mythical. He did not say, "Watch me; one day I will be crucified and I will be raised from the dead. I'll impress you! Let me perform a miracle for you, and I will show you that I am a better god than any other god." What is the greatest commandment? We can figure it out if we will think. It is to love the Lord, your God, with all your heart, mind, soul, and strength, and to love your neighbor as yourself. We may have thought that for a long time, but it is so obvious that we tend to overlook it.

When Paul went to Mars' Hill, he took on the Greeks on their home ground. He spoke as a Greek, saying, "I'll give you my myths and you give me yours." That didn't even challenge them. "What do you mean?" they asked. "Are we to believe in your God because a dead man walked around? Why, look at all of our gods and everything they can do!"

Later, Paul spent some time in Corinth. After he left, he wrote a letter to the Corinthians. Perhaps Paul was getting to know Jesus' teachings better by this time. It seems to me that somewhere along the line he had developed a better understanding of the ethical teachings of Jesus. Where does he cast his arguments now? "Though I speak with the tongues of men and of angels . . . though I can understand all prophesies . . . though I become so devoted that I even give my body to be burned; though I can do all these things that you might admire, and have not love, what does it profit me? Nothing." What happened to Paul? Now, not only had he been converted to Jesus, but at some point he had learned something about Jesus' mind. "And now abide these three things, should everything else pass away: faith, hope, and love, but the greatest of these is love." Paul was coming into his own; that is what Jesus taught, that is what Jesus lived, that is who Jesus was. However, that is not what Paul said to the Athenians.

We are aware of myths, and realize they have their place. A myth may be true or false, fact or fantasy. A myth is a traditional story form, usually employed to explain something. We all have myths and we need them. We may have a myth about our children, our parents, or ourselves. Our myths may or may not be factual; that is not important. What matters is whether they help us or hinder us.

While the image of warring gods was not unusual to the Greek mind, and is not unusual to some of us today, I would like to offer another suggestion: We need to have a battle of ideas, rather than a war of the gods. Let us allow one idea to work against another.

Jesus did that repeatedly. He said, "If they are not against us, they are for us." When asked a question, he used an idea to deal with someone. He did not attempt to win by force. On the other hand, what do we do? We want to say we can win. We proclaim Christianity to be better than every other faith. We go out to do battle. We claim the Christian faith is superior to the Jewish faith, the Moslem faith; and other faiths claim their superiority in like manner. If there is a God somewhere, a conscious, intelligent God, a God more mature than we ever could be in all of our lives, do you suppose that God rejoices to see one religion pitted against another? Do you imagine that God really wants to be right? If you are a parent and one of your children is in trouble while another is doing well, do you rejoice? Of course not! You will be with the child that needs you. It is not a question of a war of the gods, one god conquering another. What matters is compassion, understanding. We don't bring someone else to our side by arguing, putting the person down, or winning.

Power is interesting; if you have it, you really won't use it. Gerald Ford was once being interviewed on television. The interviewer said, "I would like to ask you two questions: What was your understanding of the presidency before you became president? And what was your understanding of it after you became president?" President Ford's answer was concise: "Before I became President of the United States, I was awed by the power of the office. I thought it was perhaps the most powerful office in the world. Then, after I became president, I was amazed at the lack of power; the things I could not do."

We know that is true. When you were a child you thought your parents were powerful. But when you became a parent, how much power did you have? Students view teachers as occupying seats of power. As a teacher, how much power do you have? If you work in an organization, you may think, "If I were the head of this company, look at all I would accomplish." Perhaps you would, but your power would be much less than you imagined it to be. Don't you suppose it is the same way with God? Think of the things God cannot do. From our standpoint, we might think that being God would be the most marvelous existence imaginable; all-loving, all-knowing. Would we want to be all-knowing when we are protected at any given moment by what we are not aware of that is happening elsewhere? All-powerful? God cannot solve world hunger. If anything is dear to the heart of God, that would be. What about world peace?

The war of the gods? Do you think the God that is wants to beat other gods or beat other religions? God probably would want to say to all of his children, "Understand me where you can, as you can." Yet, our culture affects us so much, and what do we do? We go from one war to another, propelled by our deep devotion. I think Jesus proposed that we let one idea combat another, and share ideas.

So often you and I will get what we want, in the final analysis. At this moment, we are pretty much what we wanted to be, whether we like it or not. Naturally we don't get all the things we want, but our personality is probably what we wanted. You and I, to a large degree, develop and become what we want to be. We often get what we want.

When we were in Greece not too long ago, we were walking through the ruins at Corinth. It was a delightful experience, except for one drawback—our guide could not speak English well enough for us to understand. Her English was no better than our Greek. As a matter of fact, her English was so poor that we could not dismiss her. We tried to say, in a nice way, "Don't come back tomorrow," but we smiled when we said it, and so there she was the next day. We walked through Corinth, and I thought how regrettable it was to be in that marvelous place, with its spectacular ruins, the birthplace of so much of the New Testament, and not even be able to understand our guide.

Some archaeologists were nearby. I decided I would try to persuade one of them to take us on a tour. But I could not find anyone willing to do so. Visiting with one archaeologist, I asked, "Why don't you come and help us for fifteen or twenty minutes?" He replied, "I can't stop." "That's strange," I thought. "This has been here for a long, long time, yet he can't stop for fifteen minutes?" We talked for a while and he told me some things that I shared with our group. Finally I asked him what he was looking for. "I don't know," he answered. "Well," I said, "I certainly hope you find it!" He had an idea what he was looking for because so much is buried in and around Corinth. He was going to find something.

We, too, are going to find something; we will almost find what we are looking for. If we decide that people don't like us, then they don't like us, from our point of view. But if we decide they do, they will probably like us, from our point of view. You and I, to a great extent, find what we are looking for. Why, then, is it necessary for some to have an angry, vindictive god that consigns people to hell? Is it only because passages in the Bible say that? But the passages say other things, too. Is it because the idea of an angry god was passed on to you by your grandparents? Maybe. Or your church? Perhaps. But you are you. How long must you adhere to a belief that is so destructive? You know what we do—psychologically, for the most part, we find what we are looking for. So when you ask me to tell you about God, I may not be telling you as much about God as I am about myself. When I speak of a compassionate God, that is the kind of God I would like to see and know. That is the kind of person I would like to be, whether I become that or not. We are going to find what we look for.

What makes one religion better than another? Is it numbers? If we hear that one church is growing rapidly, some might say, "Ah, they must be right; look at what is happening to them!" Suppose we hear that church is losing members. Then the refrain might be, "It must not be of God because it is diminishing." Do we think numbers make the difference? If that is true, then Jesus was not the Lord. If numbers are the prime factor in determining whether something is right, then Jesus was not the Lord and Savior, because his numbers diminished. His followers left him; he wound up with just a mere handful of people at the cross.

Does our devotion determine whether something is right or wrong? Our devotion may be important to us, but does it make anything right? Of course not, nor do numbers.

After all is said and done, what would make a religion right? Rightness is not determined combatively; not by the insistence that the Christian is better than the Jew or the Jew better than the Moslem; not that at all. Jesus transcended time; his mind was so keen that he could not be confined to an era. He was far too intelligent for that. Jesus' goodness came out of his brilliance. He understood to the degree that goodness was natural for him. "Why not love?" he asked. "Why not have compassion?"

What makes one religion right? Not its ability to conquer others. Jesus might have said, "If my kingdom were of this world, I would fight too. But I don't think like that." Then what does make a religion right? The answer is found in what Jesus taught. Suppose we are Christian and we persuade ourselves that the long arm of God, the might, is what is important. Then we can smash people to bits who disagree with God, through Jesus Christ, our Lord and Savior. We will win, we think, we will triumph at the end of the world, and we will be called up to heaven. Suppose we really convince ourselves that is of God, and then one day, after we have stopped shouting, there is a whisper from someone who says very clearly, "I am in another faith."

"Blessed are the meek; blessed are the merciful." Isn't that universal? Suppose that is said to you by a Jew—and it was. Suppose it is said by a Moslem or an atheist. Doesn't the world need to hear those words? Jesus taught an ethical understanding of God, not trying to confine it to one religion, but trying to let it loose in the world so it might lodge in every religion. What makes one religion better than another? Quite simply, it is the ethic of love.

Quite obviously, we do not create God. What we do create is a concept of God, or we accept an inherited one. We conceptualize in almost every area of our lives. We have a conceptual understanding of our families, of America, and of ourselves. What does it mean to be a friend? Our answer to that question would not necessarily be an accurate definition of friendship; but our answer would reveal our idea of what it means to be a friend. And so it is in regard to religion—we have a concept of religion. I believe one of the greatest things Jesus did was to give us an awareness, a concept, of what God is like. Regrettably, we took his teachings and ran them through our mill, until they came out almost as if he had not taught.

You and I will develop a concept out of our own understanding and experience. For instance, someone we trust may hurt us; if that happens several times we may decide we cannot trust people. Whether true or false, our concept is fashioned from our own experience and perception. The Greeks also did that. That is the genesis of Greek mythology and, to a great extent, that is how the Jewish faith came into existence.

The Greeks asked questions, and then they supplied answers, often through their mythology. They used their gods to satisfy their inquisitiveness. They asked, "Where did wisdom come from?" To answer their question, they began to tell a story. They said when Zeus' first wife was pregnant, someone prophesied to him that their child would be a son who would grow up and have more wisdom than his father, Zeus. That threatened the god of gods, so Zeus swallowed his wife and their unborn child. That is rather gory, is it not? Then one day, as the legend goes, Zeus was walking by the side of a river, and he developed a terrible headache, whereupon another god appeared and split Zeus' head in two and Athena, the goddess of wisdom, sprang full-grown from his brain. The Greeks had decided that wisdom came from the mind of Zeus. Who, we wonder, would be credulous enough to believe that wisdom came from the same god who swallowed his wife and child?

Yet we don't have to think very long before we see a similarity between that legend and the story of Adam and Eve—Eve was taken from the rib of Adam. You see, once an idea has been incorporated into your culture, your faith, it becomes believable, regardless of whether it is fact or fiction. The ideas and customs of others can seem so strange to us, while ours seem utterly natural. We find it preposterous that a god would swallow his wife with child, but perfectly normal and natural that a woman would come from the rib of her husband. Once you and I accept that, it makes sense to us—even if it isn't sensible.

When the Greeks wondered how Athens got its name, they devised another myth to satisfy their curiosity. Poseidon was their god of the sea, and hardly anything was more important to the Greeks than the sea. It was their highway, their life's blood. It allowed them to travel and brought trade to them. Hence, Poseidon was a significant god. Some of the people decided that their greatest city should be named "Poseidon" to honor this god who had done so much for them. Others thought of Athena, a goddess who was lovely, a goddess of wisdom; she had given them the olive tree. The olive tree was very significant to them—its wood and fruit were vital to their way of life. Athena's proponents won after much discussion, and today we call that city Athens.

People looked out and saw things, they asked questions, and then they tried to answer them in a way that would explain the situation that existed. The Jews did this, the Christians do it, Americans do it. Today we may have greater knowledge, increased understanding, but that is still how we function. We question something we see and often, out of our experience, out of our understanding, or out of our education, we form a concept. And once we have a concept, we often treat it as a fact, whether it is or not.

A recent newspaper article reported the story of a young boy who was caged by his father. When the authorities were notified, they went to the home and found the boy in a cage, in a hot, dark room. His sister was locked in her bedroom, the father was not there. One of the police officers, a professional in child abuse

103

cases, said it was the most inhuman condition he had ever seen. They opened the cage immediately and asked the boy to come out, but he cowered, refusing to budge. When one of the men asked why he would not come out, he said, "Because my daddy told me not to." Think of that! His father was his problem; his father was gone, yet the child refused to accept help. The boy had a concept of authority, a concept of right or wrong. He probably thought, "My dad must love me, even if he abuses me. He told me to stay here, so I must." The boy's concept had taken hold of him, and he treated it as reality, although it was not.

Now, let us consider this idea—our myths, our stories, create our culture. And we all have stories that we tell, do we not? We grew up with stories.

When I was very young, my great-grandfather stayed with us for some time. He had been born in Mississippi before the Civil War. Listening to my great-grandfather, my impression was that the only way the Yankees, as he called them, ever won a battle in the war was by sheer accident. My understanding of the Civil War was, to say the least, one-sided. My great-grandfather told many stories. One of them was of how his mother played "Dixie" on the piano in their parlor when the Yankees came in the door. When he would say "those Yankees," it was almost a curse. According to him, they cut the piano to pieces, while his mother played "Dixie." When told that part of the story, I almost wanted to stand up and salute. In all honesty, I'm not even sure there was a piano in their house; but there didn't have to be. That was a story we told in our family, and his mother playing "Dixie" on that piano was much better than just whistling "Dixie," wasn't it? You have similar stories in your family, and you pass them from one generation to the next.

The myth does create the culture. What myths do we have in America? What myths do we have in Christianity? One is that God is only interested in the Christian. While I grew up with that idea, I don't think I believed it even as a small boy. I hope you don't put any credence in it. If that were the case, what kind of a God would we have? If we believed that God only wants the Christian, that God and Jesus are both white, and that God prefers America, isn't that egotistical, especially when we espouse humility? What do you think Jesus would say about our demand that we be the most important? Naturally, we should be the best we can be, but must we eclipse others?

Among the many myths that we hold about ourselves, a prevalent one is that we are inept and undeserving. Perhaps we grew up thinking we never did anything right. That feeling was not taught to us; it came to us by osmosis, perhaps because we thought we were constantly being corrected. We never seemed to measure up. If a good word was spoken to us, it did not register. Such an experience would make us feel unworthy. Then, later, if someone compliments us, we think, "He doesn't know me very well." Once we have a concept of ourselves, an understanding, an awareness, we treat it as fact. And, very much like the abused child, we refuse to come out of the cage, because someone put us there. A friend may come and try to open it for us, but we say, "I can't leave."

We also create a conceptual understanding of God. Today the issue is not, "Do you believe in God?" but, "Do you believe in a vengeful God of power and might, or do you believe in a compassionate God of love and mercy?" So frequently, the God I hear preached on television and radio is the kind of God that I do not believe exists. I would ask that all of us might be like Shadrach, Meshach, and Abednego, vowing, "I am not going to believe in a God like that, even if you torture me." What kind of a God do you believe in?

Our myths, our concepts, can be advantageous to us. Have you ever consciously made an effort to recall a significant experience, one of your own personal myths, that would strengthen you? This has been beneficial to me.

Years ago, I was very ill for several weeks. During that period, I was unconscious part of the time. Then, after several days of being critically ill, in the spring of the year, I recall something which may or may not have happened: I remember hearing birds singing outside my window. I don't know for a fact that any birds were there, and I don't know if birds can sing as loudly as I thought they did. All I know is that their singing was real to me, and it gave me a feeling of security and comfort. I thought, "Everything is going to be fine. I am waking up, and I am going to be all right." All I can truthfully say is that every spring since then, when I hear birds sing, I am reminded of that experience. Whether that event actually happened or not is not important; what is significant is that, in my mind, there was an awareness that made a difference to me. Go back in your life and recall an incident that gives you strength.

Judaism did that. At one point in their history life was so difficult for them; the Jews felt threatened. And Shadrach, Meshach, and Abednego, representing the Jewish people, were asked, "Are you going to worship the golden idol that Nebuchadnezzar has built or not? Worship that idol and you will go free; just kneel down. But if you do not, you will be put in a fiery furnace." Today, the counterpart to that question is the theological query, "Will you worship the God with the powerful, strong arm? Believe in this God and you may go to heaven, but if you don't believe in this kind of God, he will send you to hell." I would rather believe in a God of love and mercy, and go to hell, than to believe in a demonic God of power, and go to heaven. Wouldn't you? Many years ago, Shadrach, Meshach, and Abednego answered in their own way. They said, "O King, we believe our God can and will deliver us. But if not, we will not worship the God you have made."

In America will we worship the God some people have conceived? Will we worship a God just like us, that votes as we do, thinks as we think, and is no bigger than we are? That is a popular concept of God; it is preached. There are biblical texts to substantiate this conception of God. But what is your concept of God?

Reinhold Niebuhr once suggested that the real problem is not atheism, the gods we do not believe in; the real problem is idolatry, the false gods we do believe in. I do not profess to know all about religion, but I will stake my life on some things, and one of them is that many of the concepts of God presented to us in our country today are false gods, no matter how much the Bible is quoted. If there is any truth to the story of Shadrach, Meshach, and Abednego—any truth at all—it is found in a quality of God.

If someone asked you if you believe in God, you'd probably say you do. The next question might be, "What kind of a God?" My hope is that all of us would reply, "I will not believe in a God of power—a God that is going to torture my child if I do not go to Holy Communion; a God that will cause me to lose my job if I do not tithe; a God that is going to send me to hell forever if I am not orthodox. I believe God will deliver me from this, but if not, I will not bow down anyway." That is the way we want to think. Go back to your past and recapture some great story from your life, your tradition, as the Jewish people did. It strengthened them; it may well strengthen you.

Now our concepts may harm us or help us. Our concept of people, of humanity, of America, of the world, either helps us or harms us. Marcus Aurelius was a Roman emperor and philosopher. Some marvelous statements are attributed to him. His approach was very pragmatic, made from a political science point of view rather than from a theological or religious position. He reasoned syllogistically that if one person has validity, all people are important; but if one person is not important, everyone is threatened. In regard to the government, he said, "We can no longer think only about just our state, the world must be the state; all people." And we think we have made so much progress when his thinking did not even stem from a religious point of view! Yet today we hear people talking about God, Jesus, and religion in a narrow, parochial way. Our understanding is indeed either beneficial or detrimental to us.

Sometime ago I visited in a hospital with a young woman who was about seven months pregnant. Her doctor and his colleagues had told her that there seemed to be no way they could save her baby. She understood that. After visiting with her for a few minutes, I turned to leave, and she said, "I can stand it, if I lose my baby, because I know it is the will of God." Normally it is not wise to counsel with anyone in such a situation. When someone is in a crisis it is sometimes better to wait. But, somehow, that seemed to be the appropriate time to me. I said, "If you don't mind, I would like to talk with you about this, very honestly." She agreed. "If you lose this baby," I said, "it is not God's will. If you lose your child and you are hurt, God is also hurt. It is as simple as that."

Before I could say any more, she reached out, took my hand, and started crying, and said, "I only said that because I thought I should, to be religious. I wondered how I was going to believe in a God who would take my baby."

109

My inclination is to say that most events, particularly world events, are not God's will. God is not in charge of everything—that is one of our dilemmas. Our problem is that we are in charge, but we are unaware we are in that position.

Since our concepts, our stories, either help us or harm us, does it not follow that if we want a better culture and a better world, we should tell a better story? A young boy in school may not think he is very bright. And, if he thinks he is not bright, that is probably the way he is going to be. But if a good teacher sits down with him and encourages him by saying, "Why, you can learn. You don't have to be afraid of making a mistake. It's fun and exciting to learn," she has told him a better story about himself. What is going to happen to him? In all probability, we can sit back and watch him grow, blossom, and develop. On a larger scale, telling a better story may be our hope.

We find that in the Old Testament, in a story dealing with such truth. "In the beginning God made everything that was made, and everything that God made He called it good." Isn't that a better story? "Every person, God called good." That is also what Jesus did. He had no political power. When we come right down to it, what did Jesus do for the world? Let us not be overly religious in replying; let us be honest, and then be religious. Jesus did not change God. He told a better story.

If you can create a better concept, you can have a better society; Jesus knew that. One day he said, "Let me tell you a story: There was a man who had two sons. One of them took his substance and went into a far country and wasted everything he had and was embarrassed to go back home. He thought he couldn't go back as a son, so he decided to go back as a servant. He started back, intending to be a servant. When he was yet a great way off, his father ran and fell on his neck and kissed him, saying, 'This, my son, was dead and is alive, was lost and is found.' The father brought his son home and they had a party." Isn't that a better story? Jesus was not talking about an earthly father, he was talking about God.

What does our world need? For one thing, it needs to hear a better story. We should present a better myth, a better conceptual understanding of God, and of people. That is exactly what Jesus Christ, whom we call our Lord and Savior, tried to do two thousand years ago, and I think that is what the Holy Spirit from God through Christ is asking us to do today.

Learning to Say Good-bye

For the most part, we do not like to say good-bye, whether our separation is to be brief or one of prolonged duration. It is difficult for us because so often when we say good-bye, we are hurt. The very word *good-bye* is somehow poignant, with its connotation of parting. Yet we find ourselves saying good-bye repeatedly, almost every day of our lives.

Jesus, too, knew what it was to try to say good-bye. At one time he turned to his disciples and said, "I am not going to be with you much longer. It is going to be different." Earlier, he had turned to them, one by one, or perhaps two or three at a time, and asked, "Will you follow me?" And they did so. Shortly after that, he said, "I don't know where I am going to spend the night." I imagine they wondered why he hadn't told them that earlier. We would have assumed some plans had been made, but there it is—a shock.

Time passed and then he said clearly, "I am not going to be with you physically like this much longer. They are going to kill me and that will be the end of it." "Don't go to Jerusalem!" Simon Peter protested. "Simon," Jesus replied, "don't let anyone know you are one of my disciples; I have enough problems as it is now." Jesus did not want martyrdom. What he said, in effect, was, "If I am going to say anything in a significant way, I need to say it in Jerusalem." That is like saying, "Turn on the microphone; get the speakers working; turn on the cameras."

The disciples were confused, thinking, "If you are the Messiah, the Savior, don't let it happen." God did not foreordain the crucifixion of Jesus; this was not a plan worked out in the mind of God; that is ridiculous. Jesus was so caught up with an idea that he was going to teach it, regardless of any consequences; and if it was the truth, it could not be destroyed.

"I am not going to be with you much longer as I am now, but, believe it or not, I will never be away from you." That was a strange idea; no wonder the disciples murmured, discussed it among themselves. They did not understand what he had said; we do not understand it either, but it is the truth. What he was saying was at least this, and undoubtedly much more: "What you liked about me when I have been with you is what I have been trying to teach. If you have caught something of the love, the mercy, the forgiveness, the closeness, these will remain with you when I have gone."

What is permanent? In your own life, what are you sure you can keep? The enduring qualities are intangible. We would expect the material to be abiding, and the intangible short-lived, yet the intangible is what lasts. Jesus alluded to this when he said, "I am not going to be with you physically, but I will never be away from you. If you have understood what I have tried to say, I will always be with you."

He was teaching his disciples how to say good-bye—good-bye to one thing so that they could say hello to something better.

Still, we would prefer not to say good-bye because it is often distressing to us. Sometime ago I was in an airport in another city, waiting to board a plane. I was sitting—kind of dozing, actually—not intending to eavesdrop, though I am not above that at all. Two men, a woman, and a child about a year old were not too far from me. I became aware of the interplay going on in their lives. One man and the woman were seated; she was holding the child. The man standing began to adjust a bag on his arm, and it became apparent that he was getting ready to take the child. Soon the woman handed the child to him, and as she did so, both she and the child began to cry. The man who took the child was ill-at-ease. The other man comforted the woman, and I realized that probably these were divorced parents, and the father was taking the child to be with him. How could they say good-bye? The child was crying as the man boarded his plane, but he wanted to be with the child, too, did he not? Sometimes the choice we have to make seems to result in a situation that is painful to all of us; nothing is right and we are caught in it. It is very easy to say to someone, "Now, just say good-bye!" Yet at certain moments in our lives we do not want to say good-bye, because it is so painful.

At other times we are unable to say good-bye because there is something we must live with. There are actually things we would like to put down and walk away from, but we cannot. These are things we are incapable of changing. That is true mentally, psychologically, and physically.

Recently, I was in west Texas working with a hospital staff who treat people suffering from mental and psychological problems. Hopefully, the time we spent together was helpful to the staff; it was a very rewarding experience for me. Throughout the day I would speak for thirty minutes or so, and then we would have open discussion. During the second lecture a door opened to my right and a woman walked in who was obviously handicapped, emotionally disturbed. She took a front seat, and when we asked for discussion, she raised her hand immediately. She was a patient and was not supposed to be a part of the meeting; she had come in unexpectedly. When she raised her hand, I said that I would like to hear what she had to say. She asked, "What would you do if you had seizures resulting from brain damage, and you never knew when they would happen? What would you do if you had to live like that?" What answer could I offer? As far as we know now, medical science can help her very little.

Some, in a situation like hers, would go to a faith healer expecting him to say a few prayers and make everything all right. We need to be realistic; sometimes we are locked into a problem. The woman was asking me an honest question and I didn't have an answer. It would have been easy for me, a stranger with some authority, to give her a glib answer. But that is the one thing I did not want to do. I wanted to talk to her as I would want her to talk to me. I said, "I don't know what I would do; I really do not know. You probably don't think you are doing well at all, but I imagine the people who know you think you are doing very well. I would like to think if that happened to me that perhaps I could handle it as well as I believe you are." And I thought, "O God, I hope I am telling her the truth. I hope I am not trying to just sound pious because there are people listening."

What would I do? I would not like to be in her situation, nor would you. We would probably pray, "God, take it away; heal me." There are times we want to say good-bye to something and we cannot, because it is a part of us. If that has not happened to you personally, it has probably happened to someone who is close to you. We all experience this to some degree, do we not?

Many of us would like to say good-bye to something when we are temporarily hurt. We may not be shattered, our whole life is not going to be affected, but we really would like to erase something from our minds. We can do this, but doing so may be tedious. If I said to you, "Think of anything about yourself except the color of your eyes," that is the one thing you will remember. When we select something in our personalities or our pasts that we want to forget, that is the one thing we recall. We are so busy remembering what we are trying to forget that we retain it. We may be embarrassed or threatened by something, and that is the one thing that keeps surfacing in our minds.

Late one afternoon I walked out of our church just as a woman drove up to the building with her son, who was about seven years old. She was a transient; she had no money. She said she needed to talk with someone who might give her financial help. The reason she had come to Fort Worth was because she had been led to believe—perhaps unintentionally—that she could find help for her son, who was ill. She had watched a television evangelist from our city, and she thought that maybe his healing service could heal her son. She had written to him, but he did not reply. He did not invite her to Fort Worth, yet she came here and tried to call him, but her calls were not returned. Perhaps he did not even know she called. I am sure I have not returned all of my phone calls; this is not a criticism of the man.

Perhaps the woman was naïve to have made the trip in the first place, but she was here and she turned to us. After talking with me about it for a few minutes, she said, "I feel like a fool; I spent so much money to come here hoping to get help, and now I cannot even talk to the people I came to see, so here I am at your church." I told her I was glad she came to us, and we gave her some money to help her get back home. Now, how will the woman feel? She will want to erase that experience from her mind. She is a reasonably intelligent person who has driven across several states with her sick child and she cannot even contact the person she hoped would help her. Not only was she returning home with her child still sick, but she was disillusioned and will want to obliterate this incident from her mind—say good-bye to it.

In order to take hold of something better, we have to let go of some things in our past. Jesus was once talking to some people, and the man we refer to as the "rich young ruler" came to him and asked, "I have kept the commandments all my life; what must I do to inherit eternal life?" Jesus responded, "Go sell what you have and give it to the poor and come and follow me." Because the man had an abundance, he went away sorrowful. We treat that incident in such a spiritual sense, as if the man should have sold everything he had and followed Jesus. If he had started to do this, in all probability Jesus would have said, "Keep some things for yourself; you don't need to get rid of everything." Actually, Jesus was testing him, not to determine his spirituality, but to see if he cared about people.

All of us would want to follow Jesus if that assured us of heaven. But that was not the issue in the story of the rich young ruler, that was not what Jesus was asking. He wanted to know, "Do you care about people? Are you going to make this life heavenly?" Jesus knew that the other life is taken care of. This rich young man's difficulty was not that he was unwilling to risk; chances are he took more financial risks than Jesus would. Jesus took risks with ideas. They both took risks; what was the real difference between them? One cared about people, and the other one didn't care enough. The rich man stood, bound to his past, perhaps thinking, "I have all of these things;

are they assets or liabilities?" Did the thought occur to him that he was going to leave them someday anyway? Could he possibly ever care enough to share? The way we see our past sometimes prevents us from accepting a better future.

When we learn to say good-bye, perhaps we can do it in a way that is beneficial—by remembering some things out of the past that are helpful. If you get a divorce, does that mean you must destroy every happy memory? A divorce does not mean there was never anything good in your marriage. Didn't you have good times, enjoy being together? So often we think things have to be white or black. When you are walking away from an experience, do not destroy everything that happened to you in that relationship. That would be unfair to yourself and to the others involved. When you are saying good-bye to something, be sensible; recapture the good, wholesome, funny, beneficial aspects of that experience.

Not too long ago I went to visit a lady who was dying of cancer; she was aware of this. Well on in years, she was a delightful, wonderful person. We had spoken of her death in the past, but this particular afternoon she said there was something she wanted to tell me. "You know, Barry, I told you quite a while ago not to pray for me to get well," she said. "It is going to be a release; I want to go on and die." I told her I understood. "Last night," she said, "I dreamed that I died, and I felt so good. When I awoke, I thought that perhaps I had died. I felt so good, until I realized that I had not died, then I became sad again."

That is about as fine a statement as I have ever heard about death. When you have lived a long life, and you reach the place where you cannot get well, you are not afraid. You know you have made mistakes, you have sinned, and you have done some very good things. Then what do you do? You recall beneficial things from your past—remember them—and allow that awareness to let you see the future.

In order to help us say good-bye, we should remember that we learn to say good-bye to one thing by learning to say hello to something else. That is what Jesus was saying to his disciples, "I am not going to be with you like this much longer. Even if they did not get to me, death would come in some form some day." Can't we learn to say hello to something better in order to say good-bye to what we are resisting? "They are going to get me; I'll be killed, but I will never really be away from you." In a religious sense, we say, "Oh, yes, there is the resurrection." That qualification is misunderstanding Jesus. He was telling his disciples that they could experience him far beyond the resurrection. "I am not going to be like this any longer, but the things within my life that you have appreciated you will have with you." Parents often experience this when their children leave home. We also experience this when someone dies.

We cannot learn to say good-bye to something by destroying it, by hating it, by running from it, or by being afraid of it—it will capture us and haunt us all our lives. Try it. Be angry at someone and decide you are going to write that person off. Why that person will possess you; anger will consume you. We learn to say good-bye to something that we need to leave, that we must leave, by learning to say hello to something else. But we can't say hello to something else if we have an attitude of destruction.

Jesus might say to the disciples, "If you are so angry about this, so threatened, so afraid, you will never experience what I am offering you; you will never understand it. But if you can recognize that they are going to get me, but that they are not going to destroy—nor can they—what I have tried to teach you; if you can understand that, I promise you, I will never be away from you." He was right; he told the truth.

Although it is sometimes difficult for us, we also need to be receptive to the surprise, to the unexpected. As children, we are almost taught that if we have enough faith, if we are good enough, and if we believe in God enough, then we can make things happen in our lives. The implication is that everything depends upon us. I don't believe that. When I am down and out, I cannot solve my own problems. That is when I need help. If we say to someone who is depressed, "Cheer up; you can do it yourself," that is the one thing the person cannot do at that moment.

Think of the good things that happen to you. You didn't bring them about; some things were luck; some things were brought about by other people. We receive benefits from many sources. We do not control our entire future. To me, one of the best things that can happen to us, in terms of saying good-bye, is to recognize the fact that the unexpected can take place. We should not take ourselves too seriously; the unusual, the hope, is always possible.

Not too long ago, in another town, my wife and I went into a restaurant just to have coffee and dessert. It was a delightful tearoom, with a warm atmosphere, so we decided to have dinner. While I was eating my soup, the waitress rushed over to our table and said, "I just found out . . . ," and I thought she was going to say, "I just found out who you are." And I was going say, in a very surprised way, that I was glad she watched our television service. Actually, she hurried over to me and said, "I just found out I served you the wrong soup."

These things happen to us; we do not control our future. We should be grateful that we don't. We do about as well as we can, sometimes we flounder, and sometimes we fail. We may say or do the wrong things, and then we feel as if we have been cheated. We all do that. Then, we have to say good-bye to some things because we want to do better; we want to say hello to something else. Life has many surprises, and some of them will hurt us. But, later, in retrospect, we see that many of the surprises have been beneficial to us. That is not false thinking. There are people who love you; various events can take place in your life. We should be receptive to those things in life that we cannot control, the gifts that come to us from life, from other people, and from God.

How do we learn to say good-bye? We don't like to do it, but at times we must. Jesus was teaching his disciples, saying, "I have been with you for a few years, but I am not going to be with you much longer; understand that. However, I want to tell you something better than that—I can really be closer to you because what you liked about me in the first place—the sharing of an idea, the thought, the personality—if you are receptive, you can have those things forever, because I will never leave you."

Learn to say good-bye to one thing so that you can say hello to something else.